IS THIS JOB MY JAM?

THE GUIDE FOR GROWN UPS WHO STILL DON'T KNOW WHAT THEY WANT TO BE

DEBORAH ATELLA

Difference Press

Washington, DC, USA

ISBN 979-8-218-64968-5

Published 2025

DISCLAIMER

Cover Design: Jennifer Stimson

Editing: Trever McKenzie

Author Photo Credit: Hayley Jean Atella

"For anyone who is tired of trying to figure out what they want to be when they grow up or what their purpose is, Is This Job my Jam? is meant for you! Deborah Atella walks you through her signature process by asking poignant questions and having you go deep. Be prepared, though, because she doesn't hold back and gives you a bit of tough love throughout the process so you can finally have the clarity you are desperately desiring. Warning: You'll no longer have an excuse for not living on purpose!"

— VAL CAP, BUSINESS MENTOR FOR COACHES

"If you would have told me I would wake up before 6:00 a.m. to continue to read any book, I would have said, 'No way.' But I couldn't put *Is This Job my Jam?* down. I read it in one and a half days and had 'a-ha!' moments in every chapter. *Is This Job my Jame?* Is a real from-the-heart, dive-deep book – how refreshing! I could feel the passion in every page and felt like Deborah Atella was talking directly to me. She made me want to get started on my actual 'jam' job immediately. 'Do the things you dream of' – I felt like I teared up a bit reading this. *Is This Job my Jam?* is a true exercise in listening to your heart in every way. Everyone who wants to feel motivated should read this book!"

— JEN PIERCE, FOUNDER OF B.A.M.

"Deborah Atella is exactly who she says she is! Authenticity is her *jam* and also her consistent life work. She is sharing her *real-life*-tested tools with the world. I'm proud to know Deborah personally and to experience her 'light-on-life' humor and intuitive wisdom. *Is This Job my Jam?* will help you find yourself while discovering your *jam!*

— SALLY YOUNG, INTUITIVE SOUL COACH

"*Is This Job My Jam?* is a must-read for anyone who wants to live a fulfilling and happy life. Deborah Atella walks readers through an easy step-by-step process of self-discovery to find clarity on exactly what they want in their life and career. Deborah's stories of her own journey are both comforting and deeply inspiring."

— JACLYN DIGREGORIO, AUTHOR AND MOTIVATIONAL SPEAKER

"Deb hit *Is This Job my Jam?* out of the park. The number one problem I see is that clients simply haven't been able to figure out what they want, what they enjoy, and what they do best. The INCH method is simple and powerful and can be used at any time, anywhere. The ability to be vulnerable and clear in the message that so many people deal with is what makes *Is This Job my Jam?* instrumental in the journey of doing what you love for real! Thank you, Deborah, for bringing this great tool and authentic story to each of us! I highly recommend you do the exercises that are recommended! It reminds me of something the great Wayne Dyer used to say: 'Don't die with your music still in you.'"

— VIKKI ROOD, CERTIFIED LIFE COACH

"This is a must read for every woman, especially after the craziness of our world right now."

— DIANNE WILLIAMS, ENTREPRENEUR

CONTENTS

For Jeff, Ricky, Jeffrey, and Gianna, the OGs of my heart!
I went all steel! I love you people!

IS THIS JOB MY JAM?

"If you don't like the path you're walking, start paving another one."

— DOLLY PARTON

"What do I want to be when I grow up? Why am I still asking myself this question? Is it even possible for me to start something new at this point in my life? Why can't I just suck it up and accept that I'm never going to figure this out? Why am I such a freaking mess? I should win an Oscar for the performance I turn in everyday! No one knows how unsatisfied, confused, stuck, bored, and resentful I am. They also don't know how embarrassed, guilty, shameful, hopeless, and ungrateful I feel for having these feelings in the first place! Ugh!"

Sound familiar?

All around you, people are posting things on social media about how they are pursuing their purpose, following their passions, and living their best lives ever. Meanwhile, you wake up every day with a nagging pit in your stomach that you just know you were made for more than your same-thing-different-day life. Everyone seems to have their lives more together than you, and that stresses you out. Maybe you thought you had it all figured out, but something happened, and now, you have to start all over. Maybe nothing happened, but what you thought would be great isn't all it's cracked up to be. Maybe you never had anything figured out, and you're exhausted of trying to make sense of it all.

Your thoughts are like a broken record. You keep playing the same track over and over again. The lyrics go something like this: "I'll never figure this out. I'm not qualified or smart enough. I need to go back to school. I'm scared. I'm too old to make a change." You're wondering why there isn't a DJ to change the track and rescue you from these sour notes. This song is not your jam! What is your jam? Who is going to help you find your jam? How much longer can you go on without figuring out your jam? You keep looking for answers and validation outside of yourself. Maybe deep down you know that you're the DJ and you have the power to choose a new song, but you're scared to make a change. Where would you even start to create a whole new playlist?

You keep focusing on whether it won't work out the way you thought it would. What if your change makes the people around you uncomfortable? What will everyone say if you leave guaranteed money and job security to go after an uncertain dream or to just try something new? These are all valid and common questions and concerns. Change is exciting, but it is also uncomfortable. Change triggers anger, frustration, anxiety, fear, and that's perfectly normal. Don't go beating yourself up if you notice this happening.

Something is pushing you to make a change with your job. If you were happy and content with your situation, chances are you wouldn't be reading this book. The truth of matter, my dear friend, is that nothing in life is certain or guaranteed except taxes and death. That's it! Everything else is subject to change in the blink of an eye! Life is short and gets messy, but there are things that you do get to control and decide. You can control your thoughts, your attitude, your effort, and your actions.

You get to decide how you spend your days earning money to support your life. Right now, you may feel overwhelmed, like you have no way to choose your job or no idea what job is best for you or your lifestyle. This is a problem, and maybe you tried to solve it in the past but never followed through, or you did and it still didn't get better. Maybe this is the first time you're ready to try to dance to a new tune. No matter what, I want you to know that I've been there, and I coached people through this. Fulfilling, positive change is possible and waiting for you to claim it!

2

ONE, TWO, TELL ME WHO ARE YOU...

"Only I can change my life. No one can do it for me."

— CAROL BURNETT

I am always fascinated by people who knew what they wanted to be when they grew up and then grew up and actually did the thing. How did they know? Why did they know? Why didn't I know? Would I ever know? Like most kids, I was told that I could be anything that I wanted to be if I applied myself and worked hard. Well, that did nothing for me because I had no clue where to even start trying to figure out what I wanted to.

Senior year of high school, my friends and I were applying to college. They were all serious about it, and I was trying my hardest to get out of it. I didn't know what to study, and honestly, I was tired of doing homework. My high school years were spent at private academy for girls that I got waitlisted for and almost didn't get into. My best friend got in. We went to school together since kindergarten. There was no way I was going to high school without her, so my sassy thirteen-year-old self called the principal of the school to find out where I fell on the list. It never once occurred to me that the average teenager wouldn't do this. I needed an answer, and she had it, so I went right to the source. She took my call but refused to answer my question. I refused to give up and called her every single day for two weeks. She took every one of my calls but never gave me an answer to my original question. On the first day of Week 3, I received an acceptance letter and admissions packet in the mail. Now, you know there was no way I was first on the list, but who doesn't let that kid in?

I spent those four years having a ball, living it up, hanging out, and making friends. I went to every school dance and activity under the sun. I was in a bunch of school clubs. I did insane amounts of homework so I didn't get grounded and loved every second I spent at that school. What I loved was my friends, the majority of my teachers, and art class. What I didn't love was putting any effort into studying, getting good grades, or preparing for college.

I was the first person in my family to go to college. I had no choice in the matter. It was expected, so I had to go. This was the mid to late 1980s. The hair was high, the shoulder pads were huge, and my grades were in the toilet. I applied to four local colleges and only got into one on the condition that I attend their summer program. It was my last choice school. I only applied there because I heard everyone got in. Well, I got in alright, and I started classes a month after my high school graduation.

Fast forward to me being in college and having to pick a major. I didn't even want to be there, let alone study one particular subject. Most of the kids I was hanging out with were majoring in criminal justice and said the classes were easy, so I picked that as my major. I begged my parents once every semester to let me quit, but no dice! I became the first person in my family to graduate from college. I earned a bachelor of arts degree in criminal justice and figured I should at least try to work in my major for a little bit to see how it would be. I got a job as a probation and parole officer.

What the eff was I thinking? I was thinking my dad knew somebody who could help get me a job and then I wouldn't have to write a resume, which all my friends were bitching about. You know how that job was? Crazy and awful! You know what was crazy and awful? Not the probationers or parolees but the system and the majority of the people I worked with. It was like a soap opera. There were affairs and drugs and thefts and threats, and that was just amongst my coworkers.

It was also the first time that I realized how quickly I could learn something. School was not my jam! It wasn't easy for me to sit and listen to a teacher lecture. That was why I liked art class so much in high school. It was all hands-on.

At this job, I picked up everything immediately and then was bored. My boss at the time was a computer whiz, and he was one of the only people in the whole building who had a desktop computer. He ran special programs detailing our revenue from collecting restitution payments and other pertinent stats. I ended up learning how to run the programs, get my own office, and became a go-to person for things I was not technically trained or qualified for. This was my first taste of being indispensable and undercompensated. That job wore me out. On top of all the craziness around me, I lost sleep worrying about the fate of the people on my caseload.

During my years there, I got married and had my first child. One day, one of my coworkers was stabbed by a probationer in the building. I quit on the spot! Nothing was worth me risking my life and not being able to raise my baby.

Luckily, I was in the process of interviewing with an insurance company. I was offered a job to come in as a claims adjuster and follow the path to becoming a fraud investigator because of my criminal justice background. I took the job, learned fast, and was once again overworked and underpaid. I quit to have two more babies and be a stay-at-home mom. I went from full time stay-at-home mom to work several part-time jobs. At one point, I owned a retail business, which was a freaking disaster! I've also worked full time and was a part of several direct sales companies until, at age forty-eight, I finally figured out what I wanted to be when I grew up!

I've never known what I was doing when I started any job. I always knew somebody or knew somebody that knew somebody that got me an interview or the job. I never *wanted* any of the jobs I had, including the retail business I owned. I just needed a job and did whatever came my way. Even though every job I ever held was in a different industry, they all had a recurring theme. Starting off, I had no clue how to do anything. Within a few weeks, I knew how to do everything and more. I got bored and took on more than I was hired for. I made no money. I helped people. People loved me. I had fun even if I hated the work. I got annoyed that I was a great worker but not making serious money. I did nothing to help myself get a raise or promotion. The whole time I was there, I had the feeling that it wasn't my jam and I was not meant to stay. Something came up, and I moved on.

Back in 2012, during one of the most stressful times in my life, a little quiet voice inside me kept saying, "Learn how to meditate, and you will feel better." A friend owned a spinning and yoga studio. I called and asked if she knew anyone who could teach me to meditate. Thankfully, she did and connected me with a gorgeous light of a woman named Ali. Ali not only taught me how to meditate, but she coached me and performed reiki. I always left feeling amazing.

Those were my first experiences with meditation, coaching, and energy work. Ali and I worked together for years, first regularly, then every now and again until she ended up relocating for work.

Over the years, I learned other forms of meditation, including transcendental meditation. Even though I meditated irregularly, I always felt the benefit whenever I practiced. In 2017, I was going through another stressful time and major life transitions. My oldest son was buying a house and moving out, my younger son was away at college, my baby girl was in high school, and the big 5-0 was a year and a half away.

I tortured myself by constantly wondering, "Shouldn't I have my life figured out by age fifty?" Why did I never feel settled? While other people my age were talking about when they were going to retire, why was I still trying to figure out what I wanted to retire from? That same little voice that whispered to me in 2012 to meditate was back. So, I decided that I was going to meditate every day for one year. I knew the answer to my burning "what do I want to be when I grow up?" question would be answered. I just didn't know how, and that was okay.

There was a problem: I was a huge quitter. I joked that I was the ultimate quitter. I even briefly quit life at one point due to a near-death experience. There were only two things in my whole life that I hadn't quit, and they were school and my marriage. Hell, I tried to quit school, but my parents would not let me. As for my marriage, my husband is a total keeper!

Could I make a promise to myself and keep meditating every day for a whole freaking year? Yes, I could... if I gave myself an out. Here's the out: I only had to do it for one minute each day. One minute! I could do anything for a minute. I put the app Insight Timer on my phone to keep track, and on April 6, 2017, I started on a journey that led to me writing this book.

I not only meditated daily but also started a whole morning routine practice. After all, why not if I only had to do each step for a minute? I have mediated and practiced a morning routine faithfully every day. Over that first year of keeping my promise to myself, answers came quicker than I ever imagined. I adopted the mantra, "I am in the right place at the right time with the right people all the time," and hot damn if it wasn't true.

Showing up for myself everyday was something I never experienced before. Spending time in silence every morning and doing things just for myself was super uncomfortable at first. Feelings and thoughts bubbled up, and I was faced with dealing with issues that I thought I had put to rest back in my years in therapy. Traumas that I buried so deep that I never even talked about in therapy kept popping up as if they were begging me to resolve them. That same little voice was back again, reminding me how much coaching and energy work helped me.

I remembered that Ali had a friend Sally, whose coaching and healing practice was exactly what I was looking for. As we began working together, it became evident that coaching interested me, so I tried coaching people a few nights a week and some weekends to see if it was my jam. It clearly was, so I invested in myself again and took coaching classes to get certified. The more energy work I received, the more it became apparent that I had gifts that I had shut down hard since my childhood. Once again, I invested in myself and added healing work in with my coaching.

I also invested in online courses, a high-level mastermind group, business and spiritual retreats, and other coaches. Some of these investments were amazing and incredibly beneficial, and some were not one bit helpful or useful. Those things were not a complete waste of my time or money because I always made invaluable connections with people in everything I did. The connections resulted in deep friendships, business associates, clients, and referrals.

The whole time I was trying out coaching people and doing healing work, I was still working a nine-to-five job where I loved my boss and coworkers. We had so much fun every day, but I knew this wasn't what I was meant to spend the rest of life doing. I was aware that I was no longer looking for anything outside of myself to make me happy. I did the inner work and was more than happy with myself. Being stuck in an office doing the same things over and over again was not for me. Whenever I worked with my coaching/ healing clients, I fell right into an easy groove. There was a peace and sense of belonging and accomplishment that I never felt before. I knew I found my jam!

I set up a plan and left my nine-to-five to work solely for myself. Now, I show up every day as the full me – no hiding or denying any part of what I do. The more me I am, the happier I am, and that causes a ripple effect to everyone I come in contact with. I love my job. I love my clients. I love myself and living and working in that full expression. I wake up every day full of gratitude for the life and business I created.

So, my dear reader friend, take my hand, and let's get to work on you gaining clarity so you can live your best life ever!

3

SING A NEW SONG

"You cannot create anew with the same ole, same ole, same ole."

— SHERRIE TAYLOR-JONES

The next five chapters of this book provide the steps of the process I use to help people gain clarity, increase their confidence, formulate a plan, take action, and find their jam! I call this the INCH method. An inch is a small measurement, but it can also be a powerful measurement. Small, consistent, aligned actions lead to massive results. Small changes are easier to achieve and maintain. Success with small changes lead to increased self-confidence, and increased self-confidence leads to you taking more action. You can't make a change or reach a goal without taking action, but you don't have to take every action all at once. Doing small things consistently also helps ward off overwhelm and stress that can result in you quitting before you reach your goal of finding a job that is your jam.

INCH stands for

- I = Identify
- N = Non-Negotiable
- C = Change
- H = Hallelujah (a.k.a. Celebration)

The steps build on each other, so I recommend doing them in order to get the full effect, but you're an adult, so you do you!

You are going to do a lot of self-inquiry and reflection throughout the rest of the book. I love anything that gives me an excuse to buy a new notebook and pen. An old school, wide ruled, marble composition book and a crystal Bic pen are my go-to favs! Maybe you like fancy gel pens and leather-bound journals or notebooks with unicorns or inspirational sayings on the front and fine tip markers. Whatever floats your boat, just have them beside you as you read so you can immediately answer the questions in each chapter.

Don't love writing or feel like it's a chore? Have Siri or Alexa take notes for you. I don't care how you record your answers just as long as you record them. The inner analysis and self-reflection are crucial for you to obtain the change you so desire. Do not lie to yourself and say you will just read through and answer the questions later. Be real; you're carving out the time to read. Are you *really* going to read it twice?

You are going to make a promise to yourself. I am going to remind you of this promise throughout the book, so it's imperative that you do it here. Repeat after me: "I, [state your name], promise to be completely honest with myself, not judge myself, and extend grace to myself throughout this process." Now, write that promise on the inside cover of your notebook or dictate it to your new personal assistant Siri or Alexa.

I have you make that promise to yourself because, as you move forward, you may feel uncomfortable answering some of the questions I pose, and you will want to skip or gloss over them. Listen, my dear reader friend, you're not where you want to be or doing what you want to be doing. You may not even have a clue about what you want to do. This is the process to help you find your jam! No one but you is going to see your answers. You aren't going to receive a grade. This isn't a test. This is you taking care of you, and if that is an alien concept for you, then definitely follow the steps as they are laid out.

INCH is made up of four steps and several principles within each step. Everything is broken down into small chunks.

STEP 1: I IS FOR IDENTIFY

How can you change anything if you aren't clear on what needs changing or fixing? You will dive deep here, and this chapter will take you the longest to get through. Since you are reading this book, I think it's safe to say your goal is to find a job that is your jam aka your dream job. You learn a breathing technique to help you trust yourself in this chapter.

Your feelings matter. The more you stuff them down and ignore them, the more they show up in other manners. I will go over different ways most people feel about their jobs, and you will acknowledge where you fit into these and powerfully decide how you want to feel moving forward. You write about what you enjoy doing, what you are good at, and how you define success.

STEP 2: N IS FOR NON-NEGOTIABLE

The term "non-negotiable" means something is not open to modification or discussion. You hear it a lot when making a large purchase like a house or car. "Price is non-negotiable!" Things like values and priorities can also be non-negotiable. Knowing your values will help you get a clearer sense of what is most important to you in your work life. A value is belief and a priority that is meaningful to you and influences your actions and reactions. You can use your values and priorities as guideposts when making decisions that lead to your dream job. You will examine and choose your top ten personal values and get clear on your non-negotiable priorities. Knowing and setting your non-negotiable priorities allows you make choices based on what's truly important to you and not what someone else feels is important. They help to reduce indecision and confusion.

STEP 3: C IS FOR CHANGE

You get your rear in gear here! You want a job that is your jam so you are going to have to make some changes. By the time you reach this step, you will have already discovered and admitted to many truths about yourself. Here, you will set SMART goals, learn about visualization and affirmations, examine ways to try things out before committing, and let go of fear.

STEP 4: H IS FOR HALLELUJAH (A.K.A. CELEBRATION)

Celebrating your small wins all along the way helps keep you motivated to reach your goal of finding a job that is your jam! You will learn why celebration is so important to lasting change. I discuss different ways for you to celebrate yourself. You will do small things consistently instead of large things all at once. Everything will fall together once you dig into the steps.

Remember your promise: honesty, no judgement, grace! Let's dig in. I am so excited for you!

TELL ME WHAT YOU THINK, WHAT YOU REALLY, REALLY THINK

"Don't be afraid to give up the good to go for the great."

— JOHN D. ROCKEFELLER

STEP 1: I IS FOR IDENTIFY

Purpose

Here is your first chance to practice what you promised: honesty, no judgement, and grace! I hear from a lot of people saying they want to know what their purpose is. What they are *really* saying is that they want to know they're doing or have done something important. The simple fact that you exist is important. You are the only you that ever has existed and will exist. I have heard motivational speaker and author Mel Robbins say that the chances of you being born are over 1 in 400 trillion. That's astounding! You are important, and everything about you matters even if you don't currently feel like that. You can do purposeful things, but your actual purpose is to live your life as you all day, every day. Now that figuring out your purpose is off the table, let's start the process of getting clear on what your jam is!

Trust

Who do you trust most in the world? If your answer isn't yourself, then ask yourself why not. If you don't trust yourself, you most likely have a habit of breaking promises to yourself. You make a New Year's resolution only to forget about in a few weeks into the year. You promise yourself that come Monday, you are going to start a diet, exercise routine, meditation practice, social media detox, go dairy and caffeine free. etc. Then, that following Monday rolls around, and you give it a go for a little while but do not follow all the way through.

Breaking promises to yourself wreaks havoc on

your self-esteem, confidence, and ability to trust yourself. If this is you, please do not berate or beat yourself up. This is more common than not, and you can change it. The absolute longest relationship you will ever have is with yourself. You have to take care of you to get what you want. Trusting yourself is paramount in decision making.

You spend so much time thinking about things, but do you ever pay attention to the signals and messages your body sends you? Your body is your wisest teacher. It knows and feels things before you can think of them. Your body sends you messages 24/7. When is the last time you realized you had an ache or pain for months before you paid attention and looked into the cause? Your body knows, so you need to pay attention to the way things feel in your body. The visceral reactions you get when some-thing sings to your soul or when something is so far out of alignment that it feels repulsive are more telling than any statistic or spreadsheet.

If you don't know what a yes and no feel like in your body, then you, my dear reader friend, are spending all your time in your head. Let's practice getting into your body right now.

I'm assuming you are in a safe place to do this

exercise. If you are not, then get into one. Sit comfortably. Close your eyes and pay attention to your breath. Put one hand on your belly and one hand on your chest. Which hand is moving, belly or chest?

Consciously breathe into your belly. Inhale through your nose, filling your belly with air so it puffs all the way out. Hold the breath for a second or two and then exhale through your mouth with an audible sigh as you empty your belly. The belly button should pull back toward the spine. Take two more breaths like this. Let those breaths go, and just keep breathing naturally. Become aware of the seat beneath you and any sensations you have in your body. Don't worry or try to change anything; just be aware.

Don't be concerned if your thoughts wander as you do this or if you never meditated before. You're doing great. Minds are made to wander; it is totally normal. Just return your attention to your breath and body when you realize it's happening.

Think about a time when you were really happy. Just go with the first thing that pops into your mind. What sensations do you feel? Where do you feel them? Now, stop and write down your answers.

Now you know what a positive or a "yes" feels like in your body.

After that, stand and shake your body off. Wiggle or jump up and down a few times. Sit again and get comfortable. Close your eyes with hands back on your body, returning attention to your breath, and do three more belly breaths.

Now, think of a time when you were unhappy – not the worst day of your life, just one in which you were plain unhappy. Go with the first memory that pops into your mind. What sensations pop up? Where are they located? Do they show up in a different spot than the happy memory? Open your eyes and write down your observations. Now you know what a negative or "no" feels like in your body. Compare your answers.

The more you practice this, the easier it is for you to trust the way answers feel in your body. Promise yourself that you will practice checking in with this breathing exercise as you build your self-trust back up!

Goal

Since you are reading this book, it's safe to say that your goal is finding a job that is your jam!

Problem

Sometimes, the thing you think is the problem is just a symptom of a bigger issue. Before you can fix or change anything, you have to identify what you think your problem is and determine if it is that or something else. Broad, blanket statements – "I hate my job," "My job sucks," or, "My boss has no clue" – don't zone in on your actual problem. You are going to whittle away at your list of complaints to narrow it down to exactly what is driving you crazy about your job. You need to get super specific so you don't end up changing the wrong thing and have to start back at ground zero.

You may realize that you enjoy the work you do but not in the environment you're in. You may decide you want to stay in your field but in a different position. You may want to completely change careers or start a business. Your dream job might not be as far away as you imagine it right now.

Lay everything out on the table, so to speak. Pretend that this book is your BFF and tell it everything it could ever want to know about your job. Feel free to vent, bitch, moan, complain, yell, curse, cry, and stomp your feet. Get all the pent-up gunk out of your system!

You might think that complaining never gets you anywhere, but the same could be said about false positivity. If you are constantly saying things like, "Well, at least I have a job," or "It could be worse," you aren't gaining clarity or making a change regardless of how true those statements are. You're still right where you were yesterday and the day before that and the day before that. Catch my drift?! You can dislike some things so much that you are blind to the other not-so-sucky or favorable parts.

I am going to ask you a bunch of questions to weed out the good, the bad, and the meh. Take your time and answer each one. If you feel like something doesn't apply, then answer "not applicable," but don't skip anything. You may not be experiencing something that I list, but you might want to avoid that in a future job. Full disclosure, these questions will take more time than the rest of the exercises in the book. They are so important for gaining clarity and making thoughtful change. Do not skip this part!

You can go through these questions in one of two ways. You can grab your notebook and pen right now and answer them as you read along, or you can read through and return later to answer. (I always suggest just doing the damn thing. Don't lie to yourself! Are you *really* going to make the time to come back?

Procrastination is just a tool we use to avoid stress. So, what's more stressful, answering some questions here and now or staying stuck and unhappy?)

I broke the questions up into categories: people, places, money, and matters. Before you start answering, remember your promise: honesty, no judgement, grace! Pause to take a few belly breaths in between each round of questions. Repeat this affirmation: "I got this." Then, start answering!

People

- How do you feel about whomever is in charge – your boss, manager, supervisor, or whatever the powers that be are called?
- How do you feel about your coworkers?
- If you are in a position of authority, how do you feel about your staff?
- How do you feel about your clientele, customers, patients, patrons, etc.?
- Do you have personality conflicts?
- Do your coworkers perform their jobs poorly and annoy you?
- Do you feel they are unreliable or dishonest?

- Do you prefer collaborating or working solo?
- Do you have any friends at work?
- Do you socialize outside of work with anyone?
- Do you feel like you fit in, or do you feel isolated?
- Are you a people person?
- Do you enjoy networking?
- Are you required to network?

Places

- What is your workspace like? Is it an office, your home, a factory, a restaurant, a bar, a retail store, a salon, etc.?
- Is your workplace structurally safe and sound?
- Is it aesthetically pleasing?
- How is your commute?
- Do you have to travel to different cities, states, or countries?
- If you do have to travel, how often?
- What is the primary mode of transportation?

- Do you want to travel more, less, or not at all?
- Where do you stay when you have to travel: hotels, motels, or AirBNB?

Money

- Do you feel you receive a fair wage?
- Do you make enough money for everything you need and want with enough overflow to save and donate?
- Are you the main financial supporter of your family?
- How are you paid: salary, hourly, commission, etc.?
- Do you get paid time off: sick days, vacation, personal days, etc.?
- Are you required to work overtime and are you paid for that?
- Do you get paid weekly, biweekly, or monthly?
- Does your employer contribute to your medical benefits or retirement plan?
- Do you carry the medical benefits for your family?

- Is there room for you to make more money in your current position with your current employer?
- How are raises, bonuses, and promotions structured?
- What is the minimum amount of money you would be satisfied making?
- Are you making at least that minimum amount?
- Did your employer contribute money to your education? If so, how long do you have to work for them without having to reimburse them?
- Do you feel like you have to stay in your job because you invested money in education or certifications?

Matters

- Do you like the actual work that you do?
- Do you like the work that you do but want to do it somewhere else?
- Are you good at what you do?
- Is your job interesting?
- Do you feel challenged by your job?
- Do you feel proud of the work you do?

- Does the way you feel about your job negatively affect your personal relationships?
- Do your personal relationships affect your job?
- If you went to college, are you working in the area of your degree? If not, do you want to?
- What's the dress code? Are you cool with it?
- What did you want to be when you grew up?
- Is your job anything like you imagined it would be?
- What's the company culture and do you agree with it?
- Do you have all the materials/tools you need to successfully perform your job and were they supplied by your employer?
- What is the main mode of communication with coworkers/ bosses/ clients/ customers/ patients: email, phone calls, Zoom calls, face-to-face interactions, etc.?
- Do you spend time doing other people's jobs?

- Do you spend time doing more manual or electronic tasks?
- Did you ever have a job you loved? If so, are there any similarities to your current job?
- What's your favorite thing about your job?
- What's your least favorite thing about your job?

Looking back at all your answers, identify your problem. What needs to change? Do you feel like the original issue/ problem/ complaint you had about your job stayed the same or changed? If it changed, what is it now?

Do your answers make you feel better or worse about your job? Do you feel like none of these things are the problem and there is something else entirely? Sometimes, people blame their jobs as being the problem, but in reality, they are looking for something outside of themselves to fill a void and make them happy. No job, house, car, relationship, or amount of money gives you what needs to come from within yourself. Happiness and fulfillment come from within you. Your job and career add to that happiness and fulfillment, but you will never feel them, or they will be fleeting if you can't find them within yourself in the first place.

Another thing that often gets missed is that people who say they are looking for their dream job are really looking for a dream lifestyle. If money were no object and your job was perfect, would you be happy with everything else about your life and lifestyle?

5

GONNA FEEL NOW

"Success is a feeling, not a series of check marks and goals."

— SIMON SINEK

You are still working on Step 1: Identify. In this chapter, you are going to identify how you feel about your job, how you want to feel, what you enjoy doing, what you are good at, and how you define success.

First and foremost, your feelings matter! I am sure there were many times in your life where you were told, "Don't feel that way," "Stop feeling like that," "You're so sensitive," or some other similar bullshit. You, my dear reader matter – and therefore your life, thoughts, dreams, ideas, feelings, goals, etc. – matter!

In my business and in my life, I see the same three feelings repeatedly show up surrounding people's jobs. They either feel happy, apathetic, or resentful.

HAPPY

If you feel happy, then you generally like your job. You're fond of most of the people you work with or for. You enjoy the physical and cultural environ-ment, the perks, the actual work, yada, yada, yada. My best intuitive guess is that this not how you feel because if you were happy about your job, you wouldn't be reading this book.

APATHETIC

If you feel apathetic about your job, then you just show up, put in your time, and collect your paycheck. You never go above or beyond what's in your job description. As a matter of fact, you might not even be doing everything you are supposed to be doing. You don't try to advance. You might spend time scrolling on social media or online shopping when you should be working. You may have been told that you need to make changes or improvements but don't. You show zero emotion, interest, or concern about anyone or anything going on. You 100 percent do not care about this job.

If this is you, my dear reader friend, what are you gaining from keeping this job that you give zero fucks about? Do you stay because the work is easy? Do you stay because it's a quick commute? Do you stay because your personal life is so stressful that at least work isn't? Do you stay because the thought of doing your resume and looking for a new job makes you want to puke? Do you stay because deep down, you like appearing disinterested and aloof because it makes you feel cool and mysterious? You definitely get some kind of buzz staying here.

Be honest with yourself. Why do you spend the majority of your time in some place doing something that you say you don't care about? Do you care more than you want to admit?

RESENTFUL

Resentful is almost always the main feeling that clients express to me about their jobs. Read this scenario and pay attention to what it brings up for you. Let whatever comes up come up! Do not judge yourself! Just feel your feelings!

You work for and with nice-enough people. There may or may not be one or two or seven jerks, but you deal with them. Your actual work may be enjoyable or, at the least, not unbearable. You may feel bored at times. As a way to advance, you start to take on extra duties, or you see people struggling and jump in to help them. Then, somehow, you end up doing work that was never meant to be yours.

You perform so efficiently and effectively that you end up doing things you weren't hired for, and your salary is not automatically increased. Maybe you get a thanks here and there or a tiny raise, but nothing substantial. You end up being the go-to person for things that you aren't even technically qualified for, but you learned how to do them, so everyone assumes they should come to you with every issue that arises. Now, you're indispensable, and some people can't function unless you are there, so you get denied time off.

You get zero perks for being awesome. You watch other people doing less than you get their every request honored and their asses kissed, yet you never go to your boss and say, "Hey I'm doing all this extra work. Can we talk about a raise or promotion or more paid time off?" You think everyone above you should be rooting for you and making sure you are well compensated and appreciated, yet no one is.

Now, you feel resentful of everyone you are helping and all those above you for not taking care of you in the way you think they should. You tell yourself, "These m'effers couldn't survive if it wasn't for me. This place would crash and burn without me. I am glue that holds this model ship together!" You tell yourself that you are a sucker, that no one appreciates what you bring to the table. You question how they could not see how much you do. You tell yourself they are selfish, and they suck!

Let me repeat the part about how you never went to anyone above you to discuss a raise, a promotion, more paid time off, or some other perk. Now, you're resentful and miserable. You're mad at yourself, but you still blame everyone else for not living up to how you expect them to act and take care of you.

Honestly, with *no* judgement or shame attached, answer these questions! What buzz do you get from being the go-to person? Does it make you feel smart or important? Does keeping everything working smoothly make you feel special? When you see other people not performing or getting things you don't think they deserve, do you feel justified in being judgmental? Do you think you would make a better boss because you would never be unaware of how hard or how much a staff member was working? Do you think you are a better human in general than the people you work for or with? Not saying no, avoiding conflict, and not advocating for yourself is people pleasing at its finest. Where else in your life do you people please?

Here's the straight talk my friend: anything you aren't fixing, changing, or leaving, you are allowing. (I am not talking about any kind of abuse situation.) That's a hard pill to swallow some days, but other days, it's freaking powerful to know you can create something better for yourself.

How do you feel: apathetic, resentful, or some other way? Make a note of how you feel. How do you want to feel at and about your job? Have you ever felt your desired feeling at a job before? What in your life would change if you could just feel that way now?

Most often, a feeling is what people are after. For example, you might say you want a diamond bracelet. What feelings does that diamond bracelet represent? Maybe it would make you feel abundant or fancy, or you think people would admire and respect you for having it. It is more about the feelings you get from the bracelet than the actual piece of jewelry. Oftentimes, this happens with people's jobs. They want to feel respected and admired or have a sense of freedom and accomplishment. The actual work they are doing isn't causing the discontent.

Make a note of what is truly causing your discontent, and make a list of how you want to feel at work. Do you do anything outside of your job that gives you the desired feelings you want from your job? Start trying things that bring those feelings into your life. For example, if you want to feel accomplished, then finish a task.

Take a deep belly breath and check in with how your desired feelings land in your body! Pay attention to what feels like a "yes" and what feels like a "no." Repeat this affirmation: "Every part of me matters! I am awesome, and I love myself!"

GOOD, BETTER, BEST!

You have things you are good, better, and the best at. When something is second nature, you often discount it as no big deal. But to someone else, it's monumental. Being punctual is a skill. You might always arrive to places on time and never give it a second thought. It's just how you are. To someone who is constantly late, you are a rockstar when it comes to punctuality.

Maybe you are a good cook and whipping up something delicious with all the leftover ingredients in your fridge is a no brainer for you. For someone who can't boil an egg, you are a talented gourmet chef. How many things are you good at that you discount? Better yet, how many things come easy to you that you don't stretch yourself to try more difficult tasks?

One of my all-time favorite books is *The Big Leap* by Gay Hendricks. In it, Hendricks says everyone has Zones of Competency, Excellence, and Genius. The majority of people spend their time in the zone of competency doing things they are competent at but not expressing their full potential. In the zone of excellence are the things you do extremely well. The zone of genius is where you do activities that are suited just to you, using your strengths and gifts. In other words, working from your innate abilities.

Make three lists use Hendricks' zones of competency, excellence, and genius. List as many examples as you can. Using my own life, here is one example under each zone. Zone of Competency: washing dishes. Zone of Excellence: cooking. Zone of Genius: reading people.

If it gets too confusing, just make a list of everything you are good at! Then, ask three to five valued and trusted people in your life what they think you are good at and what they come to you for. Do not ask anyone who stresses you out, criticizes you, or makes you feel bad about yourself. Compare the lists. Do your loved one's assessments shock you? Did you learn anything new about yourself?

What do you love to do?

Make a list of everything you love to do. Include the things that you may not have done in years but still love. What do you love most on that list? What makes you lose track of time? What feelings do these things give you? Think back to when you were little. What did you love to play? What did you want to be when you grew up? What feelings came up? What things came easy to you and what did you struggle to learn?

When I was little, I loved playing with dolls, reading books, putting on shows, and playing card and board games with my sister and cousins. I was obsessed with understanding other people's points of view, feelings, and roles. I created elaborate backstories to every adventure I took my dolls through. I would even plan out how they would feel in the clothes I dressed them in. Whenever I played cards or board games, I knew who was cheating by watching my opponents' faces and actions. I could feel when they were hiding something. Growing up, I never thought that being able to know who was lying or why they acted a certain way could be a job. I didn't know what intuition was and never heard the words empath, clairaudient, or clairsentient, yet I've always possessed those gifts. As a coach and energy practitioner, I listen to my clients and feel when they are holding back. Understanding what makes someone tick and helping them turn that into what they've been longing for, be it a job, a relationship, etc. is one of my biggest joys!

What do you already know?

Chances are that you've taken classes, earned degrees or certifications, and have had some kind of trainings in your life. Make a list of all the trainings, certifications, degrees, educations, and skills you already have. What about them relates to what you love to do? Are any of your skills, degrees or certifi-cations, transferrable?

Put It Together

Look at all of your answers and see if you find any patterns. Just because you are excellent at some-thing doesn't mean you have to turn it into a career. I am an excellent cook. I also love to cook, and it brings me great joy. However, working in a restau-rant or catering business is completely unappealing to me, so I would never make cooking my job. What are you great at? What do you love? Do the things you love bring in your desired feelings? Do you already have the training for this ideal job, or would you need more? Could you make that thing your job? Don't get caught up in the logistics right now. If money and time were no object, would you make that thing your job? Is it your jam?

SUCCESS

Success is subjective. It means something different for everyone. Merriam-Webster defines success as the attainment of wealth, favor, or eminence. What's your definition of success? You have to define it to know if you've achieved or felt it or not. When in your life have you felt successful? How important is it for you to feel successful?

Take a big belly breath right here. Check in with yourself. How do your answers make you feel? Repeat this affirmation: "I am a genius at identifying what I have and what I want! I love me!"

6

NO SCRUBS

"Your future is not determined by chance. It's deter-mined by choice."

— MEL ROBBINS

STEP 2: N IS FOR NON-NEGOTIABLE

You have needs and wants in your life. Some you are willing to give up or alter and some you are not. Knowing what is absolutely non-negotiable for yourself will reduce confusion and help you make better, aligned choices and decisions. Are you clear on your non-nego-tiables? Go through each of these categories and take note of your answers. Pay attention to how answering the questions makes you feel.

Values

One of the most interesting things I run across with people is they are completely unaware of their personal values. When I ask, "What are your values?" I am always met with a blank stare or the words "my values" repeated several times. The standard roll-off-of-the-tongue answers are family, honesty, or loyalty. Most people value those things, but they stop there and never ponder what else they value or whether their employers'/ companies'/ coworkers' values align with theirs.

If you are someone who values open-mindedness but work for and with people who are closeminded, then good luck bringing up and implementing any kind of a change. If you value equality and diversity but every time someone new gets hired, they look just like everyone already working there, what does that tell you about the way equality and diversity is valued there? Are you willing to compromise what you value and bite your tongue so hard it bleeds every day?

If you aren't clear on what your values are, then

do a quick Google search. Write down your top ten values. Does any part of your current job violate these values? On a scale of one to ten, with one being the lowest priority and ten being the highest, how important is it to work with or for people/organizations that uphold your values?

Priorities

A priority is something that is more important than something else. How clear are you on your work and life priorities? As you go through the priorities I've listed below, add and examine anything else you want. Check in with your yes/ no breath to help with determining your priorities.

Salary

Let's talk money! You need it. You work, and you receive money in exchange for that work. It comes easily to some, and others struggle their whole lives. I am not going to get into money mindset here, but I do recommend reading *It's Not Your Money* by Tosha Silver or *Sacred Success* by Barbary Stanny if you have any money mindset issues.

You did a lot of uncovering about salary in

Chapter 4. Go back and look over your answers and use the one to ten scale to rate what is your non-negotiable, highest priority about salary.

Schedule

I worked almost every single night and weekend for over three years. When I heard people saying things like, "TGIF!" or talking about their weekend plans, I wanted to punch them. My schedule is one of my top work priorities. I value my time because I know what it is like to not have any control over it.

Are you happy with your current work schedule? If not, what would you want to change about it? Does 9:00 a.m. to 5:00 p.m. work for you, or do you prefer 7:00 a.m. to 3:00 p.m.? Do you like knowing your schedule ahead of time, or are you okay with it changing week to week? How do you feel about working nights, weekends, or holidays? Get clear on your preferred schedule. Rate schedule on the one to ten scale.

Corporate Culture

Knowing what type of corporate culture you prefer ties in with knowing your values. Do you prefer working on teams and being friends with your coworkers outside of work? Do you value fast paced and competitive settings? How do you feel about high employee turnovers? Do you prefer having a defined title or everyone doing whatever needs to be done with no clear hierarchy? Doing a little research about the corporate culture before you apply for a job could save you from some big headaches later. Rate corporate culture on the one to ten scale.

Other Considerations

- The job is stimulating.
- You can learn new things and develop your skill set.
- There are opportunities for growth with the company.
- You maintain work/ life balance.
- Location is favorable.
- There are network development opportunities.

Rate these and any other priorities you have on the one to ten scale. What are your top three biggest non-negotiable priorities?

Take a deep belly breath and repeat this affirmation: "I am my biggest priority."

7

ROCK ON

"Success seems to be connected with action. Successful people keep moving. They make mistakes but they don't quit."

— CONRAD HILTON

STEP 3: C IS FOR CHANGE

I believe the age old saying that *knowledge is power* is bullshit. Knowledge is information. You just compiled a ton of knowledge about yourself, some of which you already knew and some of which may have surprised, thrilled, or annoyed you. Unless you put the knowledge to use, nothing in your life will change. The power is in what you do with the knowledge and the actions you take.

I always say, "Nothing changes if nothing changes." I have no idea where I heard that saying first, but it gets my rear in gear all the time! People say they want change but then do absolutely nothing to move the needle to make things happen. They keep playing the same song and never change the record! It is true that change can feel super difficult, but does staying in a job you hate feel juicy and delicious? Does constantly beating yourself up because you haven't figured out what job is your jam feel fun? Ever seen those memes comparing hard stuff? They go like this: "Getting fit is hard. Being unfit is hard. Being in broke is hard. Being financially responsible is hard. Trying something new is hard. Staying stuck is hard. Choose your hard."

Only you can choose your hard and change. Will you sit on all your knowledge; stay stuck, miserable, unappreciated, underpaid, unvalued, burnt out, or bored; and stew in that familiarity? Or will you bust a move and accept that change may feel unfamiliar, scary, and uncomfortable for a while as you take action? Remember, this process is named INCH because small, consistent changes lessen overwhelm and stress but lead to massive results!

You might be wondering how you even start putting all your information into action. One way is to make a SMART goal.

SMART GOALS

SMART goals were developed by George Doran, Arthur Miller, and James Cunningham in their 1981 article "There is a S.M.A.R.T. way to write management goals and objectives." Setting SMART goals squashes overwhelm.

- S = Specific. What is your goal specifically? It doesn't say general; it says specific! Here is one of the biggest mistakes and causes for overwhelm: people go too big and broad.
- M = Measurable. How will you measure your success or achievement?
- A = Attainable. Can you achieve your goal with the tools you have? If not, what do you need?
- R = Realistic. Can you realistically reach this goal?
- T = Timely. Do you have a timeline for meeting this goal?

SMART Goal Examples

Here's a SMART goal for someone with absolutely no idea what they want to do: "Identify two possible career paths I am interested in by the end of next month to help me narrow down my job search." Let's break it down.

- "Identify two possible career paths I am interested in" (Specific, Measurable, Attainable)
- "by the end of next month" (Timely)
- "to help me narrow down my job search." (Realistic)

Here's an example for someone who is starting a business: "By the end of this month, I will register my business name with my local government and apply for an employee identification number through the IRS. These are necessary steps in starting a business, and I can't open a business checking account without them."

- "By the end of this month," (Timely)
- "I will register my business name with my local government and apply for an

employee identification number through the IRS." (Specific, Measurable, Attainable)
- "These are the necessary steps in starting a business, and I can't open a business checking account without them." (Realistic)

Here's an example for someone who wants to advance in their current job but needs more training: "I will enroll in a twenty-hour online skills training course and complete at least 50 percent of the coursework within five weeks to develop the skills I need to advance in my position."

- "I will enroll in a twenty-hour online skills training course" (Specific)
- "and complete at least 50 percent of the coursework" (Measurable)
- "within five weeks" (Timely, Attainable)
- "to develop the skills I need to advance in my position." (Realistic)

Set your SMART goal. How does it feel when you stop and take a belly breath and check in with your body? Pay attention to make sure you are getting a yes/ positive feeling.

TRY IT OUT FIRST

Changing jobs or careers is a huge decision. Don't be afraid to try things out. I understand that most people do not have the privilege of just up and quitting their job to try something new, and there are ways to try things while keeping your current paycheck. Maybe you identified something that you think you might like to do, but it feels too risky to quit your job and do this completely new thing. Identify at least one person in the field/ job you're interested in. Connect through social media if you don't know them or don't have anyone to introduce you personally. Can you ask for a Zoom meeting or invite them out to coffee or lunch, your treat? Interview people. Make sure you are prepared when you meet with them and send a thank you note or email afterwards. Look for intern and volunteer opportunities. Talk to a recruiter. Look for networking opportunities. Get creative!

In Chapter 2, I told you that I spent time coaching people for a while before I decided if it would be a good career move for me. In most of those cases, I volunteered my time or traded services with people just to get the practice. Back when I had my retail business, people would always tell me that they dreamed of working in a store like mine. I offered almost every one of them the opportunity of coming in and shadowing me for the day to see if it was something they really wanted to do. Could you shadow someone for a day?

If you are still struggling with trying to choose something new, then taking an online career test is an option. These can help clarify your interests, skills, and personality types. They usually provide you with a list of occupations that could be a good match once you've finished them.

FAILURE

Failure, like success, is subjective. Dictionary.com defines failure as lack of success, an act of failing or proving unsuccessful. How do you define failure? Many people fear failure yet don't clearly define what it means to them.

I don't fear failure; I fear regret. I don't want to get to the end of my life and look back and never know how something I wanted to do could have turned out. I want to know how it turned out! I don't want to think I was too scared to try. I honestly don't look at anything that I have ever done as a failure. Some things certainly turned out unfavorable, but I either learned a lesson, got a great story from it, or found a blessing in disguise.

Let's use my meditation practice as an example. I sit and meditate first thing every morning. Some days, I get right into it, and I feel great. Some other days, my mind is wandering, and I can't settle in. That's okay. The only way I can fail at meditating is by not meditating at all. My simple act of trying counts as success to me. Don't be afraid of getting things wrong or doing them messy.

UP YOUR SKILLS

Do you have the skills needed to do something new? If not, what do you need to do to acquire or learn them? Do you need to take a class or several classes or get a new degree or certification? Are you going to let these things stop you? Maybe you feel like it would take a long time for you to obtain these new skills. Time is going to pass whether you take the classes or not.

Imagine this: the class you want to take will end two years from now, and you don't know if you should do it because two years feels too long. Pull the calendar out on your phone, scroll to that date two years into the future, and schedule this "finished class." Now, think about how you will feel two years from now when you see that notification pop up. Will you be celebrating the completion of your class and that got you your dream job, or will you be pissed off because two years flew by and you are still stuck doing the same old thing?

VISUALIZE

Visualization is a powerful tool in creating change. Visualization involves picturing in your mind something that you want. Picturing the outcome of it before it actually happens. Many people think they can't visualize because they don't see clear pictures in their mind like you would if you were watching a movie. Not everyone sees things so vividly like that. I don't see things vividly; it's more that I get a sense of things and know I am seeing them. Try this out. Picture the door that you use to enter your home. It could be the front door, back door, garage door, lobby door of an apartment building. Whatever it is you know what it looks like. Now, close your eyes, and imagine that door being painted a new, bright color, like orange, fuchsia, or fluorescent green.

Open your eyes. Did you picture it? Was it a clear picture or just a sense and a knowing? Now you know how you visualize!

Whenever I want something, trying to reach a goal, or am creating something new, I spend time visualizing the outcome before I have it. Albert Einstein said, "Imagination is everything. It is the preview for life's coming attractions." There are numerous studies and resources that say our brains don't know the difference between what is real and what is imagined. Visualization is known to help improve performance. Your creative subconscious is activated by visualization. This provides creative pathways and ideas to help you reach your goals. Visualization helps to boost your confidence. Picturing yourself achieving the goals such as landing your dream job makes them more tangible and you start to believe in your ability to do it and therefore increase your confidence!

Close your eyes and imagine yourself working a day in your dream job. Picture everything: what you're wearing, who you're with, what you're doing, where you are, and how it all looks feels and smells. Let yourself feel the ways you desire to feel and be treated at your dream job. Picture your commute. Was there traffic? Did you drive or take the train or bus? What did you have for breakfast and lunch? Did you have coffee or tea at your desk? Did you chat with coworkers or clients? Picture every single thing about a day at your dream job that you can come up with. Practice visualizing daily. It only takes a few moments, and you can even do it without closing your eyes while you are doing mundane tasks like showering or doing dishes.

AFFIRMATIONS

All throughout the book, you've been repeating affirmations. Affirmations are positive statements that you repeat to support the change you are making. They help you to challenge and overcome negative or self-sabotaging thoughts. By repeating an affirmation often, you end up believing them. They are a powerful tool in affecting change! The secret to making affirmations super powerful is to add emotion to the saying. Just going around uttering "I am confident" without ever letting yourself feel confident is not going to help. Let yourself feel the desired emotion attached to your outcome. Then create a statement to go with the emotion. Say and feel together! Whenever I am working on a new goal or want to increase my confidence about something, I set timers on my phone with the affirmations as the alarm labels. For example, at 10:00 a.m., I have an alarm that says, "I am confident in my abilities."

Take a big belly breath here and repeat the affirmation: "I conquer change with ease and grace."

8

CELEBRATE YOURSELF, C'MON

"Acknowledge all of your small victories. They will eventually add up to something great."

— KARA GOUCHER

STEP 4: H IS FOR HALLELUJAH (A.K.A. CELEBRATION)

I hear you, "Celebrate? What is this chick talking about now?" I am talking about patting yourself on the back, high fiving yourself in the mirror, shaking your groove thing and doing a little happy dance, and telling yourself you are a badass superstar who did this process well! You were celebrating yourself every time you repeated the positive affirmations that I gave you.

I celebrate myself constantly. As soon as I complete something, I celebrate in some way. My main and favorite form of celebration is happy dancing. Dancing is my jam! Did I celebrate after I wrote every chapter? You bet your sweet bippy I did. I danced, twirled, sang, fist pumped, kissed my husband, texted my daughter and sister, and kept typing.

When it's time to celebrate, it's time to celebrate, and I don't care where I am I do it. I will kick my heels up anytime, anywhere! Ask one of my kids, and they will rattle off an embarrassing moment of me dancing somewhere. I do not care what anyone thinks! I care what I think and what is going to get me to the next best level of my life. Celebrating my wins, no matter how big or small, helps me get there!

Take a big belly breath here. On the exhale, think about the happiest birthday you ever had. Let the feeling of celebration fill your body. I bet a big smile came across your face. Linger there for a few moments, then come back. Most people only allow themselves to celebrate themselves on designated birthdays or holidays if at all. They're accustomed to celebrating other people, but they feel weird or self-conscious when doing it for themselves. The longest relationship you will ever be in is with yourself. Be nice to you and celebrate you!

When you are constantly focusing on completing things so you can just get to the next task, you never feel accomplished, and burn out quickly sets in. When you pause after each step, acknowledge your work no matter how great or crappy, and celebrate, it keeps momentum going. You can experience satisfaction when completing something instead of thinking about everything you have to do as if it were strung in a never-ending strand of tangled up Christmas lights. You can't find the beginning or the end of the strand to start unraveling. It looks hopeless and like you'll never be able to get it all undone in time to hang them.

My dear reader friend, this is what you are doing to yourself by not celebrating yourself. You are in a tangled-up loop of task after task, no beginning, no end, just task. Celebration builds resilience and increases our confidence. It pumps up our positive emotions and helps us handle stressful challenges in our lives. Once our nervous system gets used to us celebrating, we are able to call up those feelings at will. As soon as I start dancing, my body feels energized.

Celebrating yourself is not some crazy idea of mine. It is practiced and taught all over because there is scientific proof to back it up! Neuropsychologist Donald Hebb used the phrase "neurons that fire together wire together" to describe how pathways in the brain are formed and reinforced through repetition. This is why another old saying *"practice makes perfect"* makes sense. The more your brain performs a certain task (e.g., celebrating), the stronger that neural network becomes, making the process more efficient each time you do that task!

This is why practices like meditation, gratitude, journaling, and celebrating are so powerful. They create and strengthen pathways in your brain for acknowledging every time you do them. The more you practice celebrating, the easier it is for your brain to process celebration!

There is no end to the ways that you can celebrate yourself. Your celebration can be big, elaborate, and expensive or small, cost nothing, and demure. I celebrate constantly, so I choose to not go the buy myself something route for the little wins and save that for the big ones like when this book is published!

Here's some ways you could celebrate yourself. You could take yourself on a date. Book a spa treatment. Make a celebration collage of pictures or images you love. Share the celebration by phoning a friend or posting about it on your favorite social media site. Buy yourself flowers. High five yourself in the mirror. Pat yourself on your back. Walk your dog. Keep a log of all of your wins. Take a nap. Go on a trip. Whistle. Watch a show. Go out to dinner. However, you choose to celebrate is perfect!

Yay, you finished reading this chapter! Start your new celebration habit right now! Repeat this affirmation: "I celebrate myself every day!"

9

ALL BY YOURSELF

"If you really want to do something, you'll find a way. If you don't, you'll find an excuse."

— JIM ROHN

Y ou just went through extensive self-reflection by answering all the questions in this book. Maybe you already started implementing changes or maybe you are just getting ready to get ready.

Getting ready to get ready is a big trap to not taking action! What is your modus operandi to reaching your goals? According to author, speaker, and coach Martha Beck, "The way we do anything is the way we do everything." Do you agree? Read this scenario and see if it resonates with you.

You decide you are going to drink a minimum of sixty-four ounces (eight eight-ounce glasses) everyday starting tomorrow. Tomorrow comes, and you start off all bright eyed and bushy tailed, ready to go. You got a fun new water bottle that holds sixty-four ounces. You fill it up and go about your day. You take some big swigs to start off with. You keep the bottle by your side all day for easy access. You grab a sip here and there. You even take a big gulp at lunch. You feel like you have spent the entire day running to the bathroom, and now it's 7:00 p.m., and you still aren't finished with your bottle. Do you finish it? Do you make the excuse that you can't drink that much and be productive too? How long do you stick with this plan of sixty-four ounces a day?

Are you in the habit of making a New Year's resolution? What's the longest time you've kept a resolution? Have you ever seen one all the way through to completion? Do you remember the promise you made to yourself in Chapter 3 – honesty, no judgement, grace? Did you keep it throughout the book?

At what point in any change you are trying to

make, do you quit? Is it at the first sign of discomfort? Is it if something starts to get expensive? Is it if someone close to you voices dissent or criticism? How do feel about yourself when you set a goal and don't reach it? Do you berate or beat yourself up?

Take a big belly breath right here. Now, close your eyes. Envision your life next year this time. You're in the same job, and it is still not your jam. Yes, you read the book; you even did the exercises as you went along. You took a little action, but when push came to shove, you gave up before you saw a result. How do you feel? Do you feel worse than you did before you even read the book, or do you feel the same? Open your eyes – literally and figuratively!

Obstacles and setbacks happen. The way you handle them matters and determines your success.

I am a recovering people pleaser, procrastinator, and perfectionist as are many of my past and current clients. These traits can easily derail the best set intentions. Knowing yourself and how you operate when making a change, operating under stress, doing things when uncomfortable, or seeing things go wrong will help you plan how to stay on track of finding a job that is your jam! Whenever I made a lasting change, I sought support. I thrive in structure, yet I struggled with setting up systems for myself, so I got help. What is your plan for when your all too familiar objections and roadblocks pop up?

Let's look at some of the most common obstacles you might encounter as you find you jam and how you can combat them!

NEGATIVE MINDSET

Negative thoughts and words about yourself can stop you before you even start anything. They can tank your self-confidence and make you question your skills, abilities, and even worthiness. The first step in combating these thoughts and self-talk is being aware of them. Release any judgement you have about yourself for having them. Focus on your strengths. Dr. Brene Brown has a saying: "The story I'm telling myself is..." Are the negative thoughts you are having about yourself in any way true or are they just a feeling or story you are telling yourself?

Maybe you tell yourself, "I mess everything up all the time, and this will be no different." Now, I guarantee you do not mess every single thing up in your life. Look for times when you didn't mess up. Even something as small as not messing up brushing your teeth! Replace that negativity with a better thought and affirmation. Try saying and thinking, "I try my best" or "I am constantly improving."

PROCRASTINATION AND POOR TIME MANAGEMENT

Do you procrastinate? Tell yourself you will just do things later and then later arrives and you still don't do the damn things? I was the ultimate procrastinator. I've heard it said by author and coach Mel Robbins that people procrastinate to relieve stress. You have something you have to get done, but it stresses you out to the max just even thinking about it.

Let's say it's updating your resume. You hate this task. You google different resume examples. You feel so much stress about doing this that you spend the next three hours watching TikTok videos. You fall asleep, and another day passes without you updating your resume and staying stuck in your non-jam job! A way to combat procrastination is to set a timer for five minutes. You work on the resume for five minutes. When the timer goes off, you can stop or choose to keep going. If you aren't able to complete the task in five minutes, you can choose when you will give it another five minutes of your time and then go for it! Another tactic is to call in reinforcements. Have someone you value and trust hold you accountable. Let them know you need to update your resume, and ask them to hold you accountable to having it done by a certain time. You can use the reward system that once you complete this task you will get yourself a treat. Think about how good you will feel when it is all done! Sometimes just that thought is enough to stop procrastination in its tracks.

How do you manage your time? Here's a fact about time. Everyone has the same number of hours in a day. How you choose to spend them influences and affects your life. Instead of saying you don't have time for something you claim to want, how about switching your words to, "This isn't a priority for me right now." How does that feel? When you manage your time wisely, it frees you up to have time to do the things you want to do instead of just the things you have to do.

OVERWHELM

Trying to make too many changes at once causes overwhelm. Breaking things down into small chunks like in the INCH method leads to less stress and more success.

FEARS

First, figure out what you fear. I told you I fear regret. Many people fear success or failure or loss. Fear is a strong force, and it tries to get you to play it safe and not rock the boat by making changes. Look at times in your life when you were successful at something that you originally feared doing. How did you push through? Repeat that! Oftentimes, you're fearing being uncomfortable and uncertain. Focus on the present and what's one small thing you can do today to move you forward in finding your dream job? Be okay with not being comfortable 24/7. Be honest with your feelings and call in help if need be.

PERFECTIONISM

Perfectionism is wanting things to be perfect or wanting to do things to be perfectly. The perfectionist will not do things if they can't do it perfectly. If they don't have all of the perfect tools, they need then forget about doing anything. This can lead to never reaching your goals! Get comfortable with doing things messy. The first time I heard Cheryl Sanburg say, "Done is better than perfect," I adopted that as one of my life's mantras.

PEOPLE PLEASING

You might not think you are a people pleaser, but you really could be. I didn't think I was, but hello, I totally was! You want to appear competent. You want people to like and value you so you do things that really aren't your jam to get praise or keep the peace. Be self-aware. Practice self-care. Learn how to set boundaries. These practices help end people pleasing.

PESSIMISTIC PEOPLE

Pessimistic people are everywhere. If you have a lot of them in close proximity to your life, do you let their opinions influence your choices and decisions? If you do, then re-read people pleasing above! Don't let someone rain on your parade. Oftentimes, people try to discourage you from making a change because they fear change. It really has nothing to do with you. Or your change might make you less available to them, and they don't want that, so they try and discourage you. Either way, stop giving other people a starring role in your life.

RESISTANCE

Feeling resistant to change is very common. It ties into uncertainty and fear of the unknown. Get comfortable being uncomfortable. Practice self-acceptance. Ease into things by avoiding overwhelm.

EXPECTATIONS

Expecting things to turn out a certain way or for people to make you feel a specific way is a recipe for disaster! If you are expecting a new job to make you happy but you are not happy with yourself, you are going to extremely disappointed. Happiness is a choice and an inside job. I make the decision every day to be happy. Some ways to find happiness with yourself is to first of all stop comparing yourself to others. Life isn't a contest. Give yourself grace and treat yourself like your best friend. When you make a mistake, ask yourself how you would respond if your best friend did this. You are a work in progress. Be nice to yourself.

You spend more time with yourself than anyone in the world!

The truth is that not everyone has the luxury of just up and quitting their job to start something new. Sometimes, you have to stay in a job because you need the medical benefits or you can't find something where you will make the same or more money. No matter what your situation is, you can always do something that is your jam even if it is not your job and it is only for five minutes a day. Some people are fine with doing a job that pays the bills and revel in their zone of genius off hours and their hobbies are their jam.

Take a big belly breath. Repeat this affirmation: "I am my jam!"

10

LIVE AND LET'S THRIVE

"Success is liking yourself, liking what you do and liking how you do it."

— MAYA ANGELOU

I wrote this book because I know there are so many people out there struggling to figure out what to do with their lives. They think they must have a job that defines them and has purpose and meaning, but they don't feel like their job or their lives meet those criteria. I hear middle-aged women especially, say, "I wish I knew what I wanted to be when I grow up," and then laugh.

I used to say it all the time too. Then, I learned how to quiet down my inner critic and hear the guidance and the answers to my questions. If I didn't hear an immediate answer, I was led to the methods that found it, like soft suggestions connecting me to the right people and the right places at the right time. These were clues dropped like breadcrumbs for me to follow. Once I followed the trail and learned to love and trust myself, I easily saw what I was meant to do and that I could actually make a difference and money doing it.

I learned how to be happy – truly happy – with myself, and I want that for every person out there. Everyone deserves to be happy and live joyful lives. I know everyone has crap that goes on, and some people have horrible things that happened to them, but that doesn't change the fact that they deserve happiness.

Most people think that *something* is their problem, and if they could just solve that one problem, then they would be happy. I wrote this book for the person whose kids are flying the coop and the individual who is suddenly alone or in a new phase of her life and feels like she is floundering. While the book is titled *Is This Job My Jam?*, the principles in the book can be used to figure out anything in your life. You can use them to figure out relationships (romantic or platonic) and self-care. You may even use this as an opportunity to consider how you truly feel about yourself and how you want to feel.

It is said time and time again that happiness is an inside job, and it is so true. Happiness is a decision. I wake up every morning and immediately express gratitude and declare that I am happy! It is a practice just like yoga or meditation.

When you feel better, you do better, and it causes a ripple effect to those around you.

It is so much easier for your life to blossom in unexpected ways if you are kinder, gentler, and more forgiving of yourself. Doesn't that sound amazing? I wrote this book to make a difference for you and show you how simple things can be. Simple doesn't mean easy; it still takes work and dedication. But when you extend grace to yourself, it makes a major difference. You deserve grace. You deserve to be happy. You deserve to feel like you matter and feel seen, heard, and appreciated.

I wrote this book to give you hope. It is never too late to do the things that are in your heart. If you have to go back to school, so be it. Just effing do it. If you need a certification, then get it. If you have to hire a coach, then hire one. Do the things you dream of. Even if they become a hobby instead of your job, so what? As long as you are happy, that is what counts.

As I said before, I fear regret more than failure or even success. I never want to look back and think, "Why didn't I try that?" or, "I wish I knew how that would have turned out if I just tried." I always just try. What's the worst that could happen? Don't look at things as failures ever. Sometimes, things don't work out the way you want them to, and that's okay. Sometimes, they turn out better than you ever could have imagined. Sometimes, you just get a lesson from them or, at minimum, a hell of a story! I would rather have tons of stories to tell than twiddle my thumbs or wring my hands in regret.

Life is short. Do the things that make you happy and the things that lighten your load and put a pep in your step. Sometimes, that's getting a new job, a new attitude, or a new pair of shoes!

My dear reader friend, you went on quite the journey over these past chapters. In Chapter 4, you started INCHing your way to figuring out your jam! You identified that you are your purpose and that you can do purposeful things. You learned what "yes" and "no" feel like in your body and identified what you needed and wanted to change.

In Chapter 5, you identified how you feel about

your job, what you are great at, what you love doing, and how you define success. In Chapter 6, you got your priorities in order. You conquered your change, set SMART goals, visualized, and made affirmations in Chapter 7. In Chapter 8, you celebrated yourself. (If you are anything like me, you were shaking your booty!) In Chapter 9, you thought about how you will handle things moving forward.

My wish for you is that you accept and appreciate that you are the DJ of your life. You choose the records that play in your head. You are in charge of making good choices for yourself. You are capable of change. I hope your confidence increases through the small, consistent promises and actions that you take. But most of all, I hope you know that you are your jam!

Never forget that you matter not only to the world but also to me!

ACKNOWLEDGMENTS

As I sat to meditate and pray early on one cold February morning, I asked God to let me know what was next and how I could serve more. I didn't get an immediate answer – no clue, no feeling, no vision, no whispers, nothing. I wasn't discouraged because I know how it works. At some point, God would let me know the next move; until then, I just kept believing that the answers would come. A little while later, after I finished my morning routine practice, I logged on to social media and saw an ad with Dr. Angela Lauria and Marianne Williamson. Studying *A Course in Miracles* is part of my morning practice, and if you know about the course you know about Marianne Williamson. I clearly knew that whatever this ad was would lead me to what I was supposed to do next. It was the answer to my prayer! I clicked the link, and I was led to write under the incredible guidance of Dr. Angela Lauria and her company, The Author Incubator.

Thank you, God. You always have my back!

Angela, you forever changed my life! Your guidance and coaching are beyond anything I ever experienced. In the blink of an eye, I went from dreaming about being a published author to actually being one! I adore you and can't wait to see what else we create together. Thank you from the bottom of my heart!

Marianne Williamson, thank you for seeing me and leading us every Wednesday afternoon.

Karmi Koen, Ramses Rodriguez, Madeline Kosten, Mila Nedelijkov, Lesley Matthews, and all of staff at The Author Incubator, thank you for all the magic you help make happen! Trever McKenzie, you, my dear, are beyond patient, kind, brilliant, and understanding! Thank you for talking me off the ledge every week! Jennifer Stimson, I love my cover!

To my Author Incubator cohort, I love and appreciate you ladies! Kelly Ruby Hanson and Laura Dill, thanks for the extra handholding!

Sonia, Adrea, Rochelle, Maria, and Amy, thank you for loving me, thinking I am funny, and being my friend! I love you all!

Ginger, thank you for never letting me get away without answering your questions and for challenging me to dig deeper! I love you and our friendship!

Ali, I am so grateful for you and the path our work together put me on! I adore you!

Sally, few people have touched my life or believed in me the way you have. I trust you with my soul! Thank you. I love you!

Mom, I wouldn't be here without you! Thank you for reading me *Snow White* one hundred bajillion times, letting me order books at every school book fair, making sure there were always books under the Christmas tree and at every birthday, and passing on your love of reading. I love you!

Clara, your influence in my life is seen in everything I do. I wrote your name in a book. Now you're immortal to the rest of the world!

Laura, you crazy, beautiful, forever young girl, thank you for always making your presence known and for sending me back that time I died! I will never not miss you.

Tommy, I love you and can't wait to see what you and Alicia build together!

Camille, my bud! Our relationship is vital in my life. Your love and support are unconditional and I love you! We are ride or die for life!

Jeanine, I love you, my sister! I can't even put into words what you mean to me, so I won't, because you know. Plus, I have you pre-edit me, so that won't work here! I couldn't have written this book without your love, encouragement, and humor! I can't wait to wear sweaters and eat at buffets with you. Thank you!

Sonny, my love! You will never not know me as an author and that makes me smile! Let's face it, everything about you makes me smile. You stole my heart and I never want it back!

Hayley I couldn't have picked a better wife for Ricky, mother for Sonny or bonus daughter for me! I am so grateful for you and our relationship! Thanks for dolling me up, taking my headshots and helping me with this book. I love you!

Ricky, Jeffrey and Gianna, being your mother is the greatest gift of my life! Your love and trust fuel me. Ricky, you made me a mom and now seeing you as a dad is one of the most beautiful sights I have ever seen. I am so proud of the man you are! Jeffrey, watching you go after your dreams is inspiring and makes me so proud and happy! I will bring you meatballs soon! Gianna, you are the girl of my dreams! I honestly don't know how I would have finished this book without you by my side. You are wise well beyond your years. Your future is so bright, and I am so proud of you!

I love you people!

Jeff, thank you for believing in me and encouraging me to do all the things I do! This book would not exist without your love, faith, and trust in me. You have held my hand on the best days of my life and held me up on the worst. There's no one I would rather share this lifetime with, and that's not just because your butt is still so cute in your jeans! You're my favorite person and I love you.

ABOUT THE AUTHOR

Deborah Atella is a podcaster, author, certified life coach, meditation teacher, and Reiki master. She hosts I *Freaking Knew It*, a podcast dedicated to exploring the power of intuition.

She is also the author of *Is This Job My Jam? The Guide for Grown-Ups Who Still Don't Know What They Want to Be*. After years of excelling in jobs that didn't truly fulfill her, balancing work and motherhood, and suppressing her spiritual gifts, Deborah embarked on a journey of self-discovery. That path led to clarity, a renewed sense of purpose, and ultimately, the launch of her coaching business. A life-changing leap of faith taught her to trust her instincts—wisdom she now shares with her clients as they navigate transitions and uncover their own truths.

Born and raised in Philadelphia, Deborah now lives in the suburbs with her husband, Jeff. Together, they've raised three wonderful children who are now grown. When she's not coaching or creating, she loves seeking out new adventures, cooking big Italian meals, unwinding at the beach, and most of all, spending time with her grandson.

Website: www.deborahatella.com
Instagram: www.instagram.com/deborahatella
Linktree: https://linktr.ee/deborahatella

THANK YOU

Thank you so much for reading *Is This Job My Jam?: The Guide for Grown Ups Who Still Don't Know What They Want to Be.* I would love to learn more about your journey and success in finding your dream job. Please keep in touch on www.instagram.com/debora hatella and share your wins (tag me and use #isthisjobmyjam).